REE

BEGIN

RLD

POWER

RIGHT

FRIEND

FOE

ERICA

WAR

PEACE

PLEDGE

LOYALTY

SCIENCE

MANKIND

TRY

HISTORY

ASK

John F. Kennedy

The Making of His Inaugural Address

JOHN F. KENNEDY

THE MAKING OF HIS INAUGURAL ADDRESS

Commentary by Roger G. Kennedy

Director Emeritus

National Museum of American History

LEVENGER PRESS

Published by
Levenger Press
420 South Congress Avenue
Delray Beach, Florida 33445 USA
Levengerpress.com 800.544.0880

First Edition 2009

Facsimiles and recordings are from the archives of the John F. Kennedy Presidential Museum and Library.

Library of Congress Cataloging-in-Publication Data

John F. Kennedy : the making of his inaugural address / commentary by Roger G. Kennedy. -- 1st ed.
     p. cm.
  Includes bibliographical references.
  ISBN 978-1-929154-37-1
  1. Kennedy, John F. (John Fitzgerald), 1917-1963--Inauguration, 1961. 2. Presidents--United States--
Inaugural addresses. 3. United States--Politics and government--1961-1963. I. Kennedy, Roger G.
  J82.D91J64 2009
  352.23'860973--dc22
                                            2009007788

Cover and book design by Danielle Furci
Additional art by Kristin Currier-Ludlow and Laura Parker
Mim Harrison, Editor

Printed in the USA

PROGRAM

Prologue
Igniting the Flame
Publisher's preface

The Inaugural Address

…as it was created
Facsimiles of the working documents

…as it was delivered
The reading copy showing JFK's emendations

…as it lives in history
Roger G. Kennedy on the sacred fire of liberty

Epilogue
Transcription of the Recorded Speech

PROLOGUE

Igniting the Flame

Publisher's preface

IGNITING THE FLAME

It drew on the words of Isaiah, the tempo of Lincoln, and the cadence of Churchill. John Fitzgerald Kennedy's Inaugural Address was in many ways a product of the Classical Age, with words that were deeply rooted in history and yet contained the vision that would enkindle a then-and-future generation. As Theodore Sorensen wrote, Kennedy "spoke to the country's nobler instincts," a statement that calls to mind the closing phrase from Lincoln's first Inaugural Address of "the better angels of our nature."

An inaugural address is an amalgam of statesmanship and craftsmanship. Expounding on the lofty ideal is juxtaposed with crossing out the word that doesn't quite work. In this book, we bring you both these aspects of Kennedy's Inaugural Address—its making and its meaning. And we invite you not so much to read about this speech as to experience it.

We suggest you begin by playing the first segment of the DVD, which shows JFK delivering his address. It will help put you in Washington on that blustery January day in 1961, where a northwest wind made the temperature feel like 7° F. You will see in color, as if you were there, what most Americans witnessed in black and white on their TV screens. That television audience was the largest in history.

The making

Then experience the intense flurry of the speech's creation. Kennedy's was one of the shortest inaugural addresses in America's history. Even so, many words went into shaping it in the final two months of 1960 and the first nineteen days of 1961. Facsimiles of various working documents show you the words as they were being molded—Kennedy's dictation of his address to his secretary Evelyn Lincoln, edits to the typed iteration, JFK's own handwritten version, and the reading copy placed at the rostrum on Inauguration Day.

Although the reading copy contained the final words for the Inaugural Address that were written, they were not the final words that John F. Kennedy spoke. So that you can see how and where JFK ad-libbed, we have superimposed his verbal emendations onto the facsimile of the reading copy.

The meaning

Kennedy spoke his words in approximately fifteen minutes, but they have resonated for decades. Roger G. Kennedy's commentary, "The Sacred Fire of Liberty," examines the reasons for this, placing the speech in the context of both its time and the country's larger history.

In addition to being a historian, Mr. Kennedy is a longtime Washingtonian who has served under both Republican and Democratic presidents (and who by happenstance shares a surname with JFK). He analyzes for us the antecedents of JFK's Inaugural Address, and shows us how a speech grounded in that moment of America's history also soared with a forward-thinking trajectory.

Once you've absorbed this commentary, we recommend you watch the DVD again—this time, including the second segment, which documents the entire Inauguration Day.

"The world is very different now," Kennedy stated shortly into his address. And so it was. But as Roger Kennedy demonstrates, it was also a time that brought us to the world we live in today. Whether you can recall JFK's era firsthand or know it only as a history lesson, we hope the experience of this book helps to bring alive his first words as the nation's president, and offers a new way to see both the mind of the man and the time.

THE INAUGURAL ADDRESS

...as it was created

Facsimiles of the working documents

A GRAND COLLABORATION

Theodore C. Sorensen served as special counsel to JFK as President and as trusted adviser to him for the ten years and eleven months the two knew each other. As Kennedy's speechwriter, Sorensen worked closely with Kennedy on the Inaugural Address in much the same way he did with JFK's other speeches: collaboratively.

Theirs was one of the most seamless such collaborations in history, and Sorensen's recollections of the creation of the Inaugural Address reveal the underpinnings of how it worked and why it did so well: "[M]uch of JFK's first dictation was based upon my early draft, and…portions of my early drafts were based upon his earlier campaign speeches, which were themselves most often works of collaboration between us, some of which drew from ideas and phrases from a variety of historical statesmen and writers."

Madeleine Albright, the former Secretary of State, called Sorensen's and Kennedy's "[t]he ideal partnership between a speechwriter and a modern president." She notes that even George Washington had help with his first address to Congress (from James Madison), as did Lincoln with his first inaugural address (from William Seward).

The Kennedy-Sorensen collaboration was built on a foundation of shared beliefs and ideologies, a reverence for the role of well-chosen words in shaping history, and admiration for the observations of great thinkers and leaders through the ages. It also helped that Sorensen had an ear honed to Kennedy's voice.

As much as a great speech is about words, an even greater force is shaping it. JFK's Inaugural Address galvanized a generation because of what he put behind the words. As Sorensen says: "his best speeches moved people not because of the grandeur of his phrases…but because of the grandeur of his ideas."

BREVITY AS THE SOUL OF WISDOM

On January 20, 1961, the day Kennedy took the oath of office as President, his Inaugural Address stood as the fourth shortest in the country's history: 1,347 words. That was by design.

Early in the crafting of the speech, Kennedy instructed Sorensen to research other inaugural addresses he admired and to do a word count of them. Sorensen's notes on this subject include these instructions: "make it the shortest since T.R. [Teddy Roosevelt]"; "eliminate I specifics" [so that JFK rarely used the first person]; and "shorter sentences & words."

Sorensen also jotted down a number of inaugural addresses whose words he would count in addition to Teddy Roosevelt's. They included those of Lincoln, Franklin Roosevelt (FDR), Eisenhower (Ike), and Woodrow Wilson. The typed note on the following page includes some of those word counts, along with the count at that point in Kennedy's address ("TCS draft"). JFK came to the presidency from the U.S. Senate—hence the Senate memorandum paper.

'61   [List for Sunday? ("SAVE wd m{nt?})]
    CASH!

Count words in draft
    "   "   " Dec '57,
FDR '41, Wilson '17, Wilson '13

A   Our objectives

Leave no copies around,
    even RNC-MP
TR & _____

— avoid _____ & eloquence

— Shorten sentences & words

— Eliminate _____ & _____

— Make ct of _____ and
  T.R (except for FDR's
  abbreviated war-time _____
  in (1945)

(Too short & text:)	Count, & Compare
FDR, 1945	Ike, 1957
TR, 1905	FDR, 1941
Grant, 1869	Wilson, 1917
Lincoln, 1865	Wilson, 1913
Taylor, 1849	Cleveland, 1885
	Grant, 1873

United States Senate

MEMORANDUM

Roosevelt	1941	1281 words
Wilson	1917	1485 words
Wilson	1913	1690 words
Eisenhower	1957	1730 words
TCS draft		1693 words

$$-413$$
$$1280$$

Shorter than Eisenhower?
Hoover
Coolidge
Harding
Taft
McKinley
Wilson's 2

FDR's 1st & 2nd

CASTING THE NET WIDE

In a departure from most Kennedy speeches, the Inaugural Address went through a call-for-ideas phase. Two days before Christmas 1960, Sorensen sent a query to ten leading thinkers of the day. The quickest way to execute such a request at the time was by "block wire" telegram.

Adlai Stevenson, who had twice run unsuccessfully for the presidency, was among those Sorensen queried. Stevenson sent a reply telegram on December 28th with the message, "Your wire arrives at most difficult time for me. I will do what I can."

Two days later he sent a three-page letter (following pages) outlining his recommendations for what JFK should include in the realm of foreign affairs. Kennedy tapped into both Stevenson's ideas as well as John Kenneth Galbraith's.

WESTERN UNION
TELEGRAM
W. P. MARSHALL, PRESIDENT

1211 (4-55)

NO. WDS.-CL. OF SVC.	PD. OR COLL.	CASH NO.	CHARGE TO THE ACCOUNT OF	TIME FILED
			SENATOR KENNEDY - OFFICIAL	DEC. 23, 1960

Send the following message, subject to the terms on back hereof, which are hereby agreed to

BLOCK WIRE

Dr. Allan Nevins
Huntington Library and Art Gallery
1151 Oxford Road
San Marino 9, California

Hon. Adlai E. Stevenson
135 South LaSalle Street
Chicago 3, Illinois

Mr. Douglas Dillon
Hobe Sound
Florida

Mr. Joseph Kraft
1148 Fifth Avenue
New York, New York

Hon. Chester Bowles
Hayden's Point
Essex, Connecticut

Mr. Arthur Goldberg
1001 Connecticut Avenue, N.W.
Washington, D. C.

Mr. Dean Rusk
21 Fenimore Road
Scarsdale, New York

Mr. Fred Dutton
1131 11th Avenue
Sacramento, California

Mr. David Lloyd
1329 18th Street, N.W.
Washington, D. C.

Prof. J. K. Galbraith
30 Francis Avenue
Cambridge, Massachusetts

The President-Elect has asked me to collect any suggestions you may have for the Inaugural Address. In view of the short period of time available before Inauguration Day, it would be appreciated if we could have your recommendations by December 31. We are particularly interested in specific themes and in language to articulate these themes whether it takes one page or ten pages. Many many thanks.

Theodore C. Sorensen
Special Counsel to the
President-Elect

- FELDMAN
- GOODWIN

9

ADLAI E. STEVENSON
135 So. LaSalle Street
Chicago

December 30, 1960

Mr. Theodore C. Sorensen
c/o Hon. John F. Kennedy
United States Senate
Washington 25, D. C.

Dear Mr. Sorensen:

In response to your telegram of December 24 requesting suggestions for the Inaugural by December 31, I will confine my comments to foreign affairs. Due to a myriad of other pressing "priorities" just now, I have had little time for this, but my first reaction is that it would be well for Senator Kennedy to include the following:

1. A frank acknowledgement of the changing equilibrium in the world and the grave dangers and difficulties which the West faces for the first time.

2. The assertion that our objective is the peace, the progress and the independence of all people, everywhere. We want to end, not prolong the cold war. Hence, all-out support of the UN, (a) as the protector of the new nations against involvement in the cold war; (b) as the ideal instrument for fostering economic development; (c) as the agency which will have to be strengthened in order that it may be able to keep the peace and enforce world law.

3. An unequivocal commitment to disarmament.

4. Recognition that the first order of business is to halt the proliferation of nuclear powers and to reduce the ever growing danger of war by accident.

5. An unequivocal commitment to the Western defensive alliance to deter aggression and keep the peace.

11

6.   Definition of the ultimate goal of world-wide cooperation on the part of the industrialized nations toward lifting the living standards of the underprivileged peoples.   However, so long as the Communists want to compete instead of cooperate, an assumption of leadership in organizing the resources of the non-Communist industrialized nations in a multilateral cooperative effort to win the non-military cold war. (Perhaps a nod of approval and hope for the OECD would be helpful.)

7.   Recognition of a special U.S. responsibility for Latin America.

8.   A disavowal of the Republican proposal to reduce foreign economic aid and a pledge to increase it, as possible, provided other industrialized nations do their share (especially Germany).

9.   A desire to liquidate overseas military bases as fast as progress toward disarmament makes this possible.

10.   Eagerness to reduce tensions by negotiation in the hot spot areas (Germany, the Taiwan Strait, the Middle East, Congo, Cuba, Laos).

11.   Perhaps a conditioned hint of re-examination of our China policy to advance controlled disarmament and reduce the danger of war in Asia.

The main thing, of course, is to create the impression of new, bold, imaginative, purposeful leadership; to de-emphasize the bi-polar power struggle; and to emphasize the affirmative approaches to peace. (In this connection, what about a proposal to put all space exploration under UN control?)

You are doubtless familiar with my report to Senator Kennedy and the recommendation of an omnibus bill to gather our aid agencies together for unified direction. Because I think this most important I would like Jack to mention it, although the State of the Union may be a more appropriate time for programmatic proposals.

I have not been able to articulate all
of this, but enclose some hurried paragraphs
which are an attempt to cover at least some
of the points, including some passages which
are probably quite inappropriate for his
address.

I'm afraid this may all be too hurried
to be helpful. I will be in Washington (at
FEderal 3-5165) Tuesday and part of Wednesday
of next week, in case I can be of any help.

Sincerely yours,

Adlai E. Stevenson

KENNEDY AND LINCOLN

Among those offering advice to JFK on the content of his Inaugural Address was Philip Graham, the publisher of the *Washington Post*. In his letter of January 5th, he was already addressing JFK as "Mr. President," and he chose as his referential touchstone Abraham Lincoln.

Both Kennedy and Sorensen were admirers of Lincoln's speeches, and Kennedy found the Gettysburg Address in particular to be the avatar of a powerful short speech. Two months after JFK took the oath of office, the White House reenacted Abraham Lincoln's first inauguration, which was marking its centenary. Carl Sandburg, the poet and historian whose biography of Lincoln won the Pulitzer Prize, delivered the remarks.

Sandburg considered Kennedy's Inaugural Address to be one of the finest in America's history. In Kennedy's can be heard an echo of Lincoln's (perhaps Lincoln had struck one of the "mystic chords of memory" he spoke of in his first inaugural address):

> Lincoln: "In *your* hands, my dissatisfied fellow countrymen, and not in *mine*, is the momentous issue of civil war."

> Kennedy: "In your hands, my fellow citizens, more than mine, will rest the final success or failure of our course."

The Lincolnesque reference was not lost on its listeners—even the *Times* of London remarked on it.

Inaugural

The Washington Post

1515 L STREET, N.W.   WASHINGTON 5, D.C.

REPUBLIC 7-1234

PHILIP L. GRAHAM
PUBLISHER

January 5, 1961

Dear Mr. President:

Years ago Mr. Justice Frankfurter gave me a lesson in
ghost-writing by showing me Seward's suggestion for the close of
the First Inaugural, and Lincoln's reworking of that close.

They follow:

(a) Seward's suggestion--

"I close. We are not we must not be aliens or enemies
but fellow countrymen and brethren.   Although passion has
strained our bonds of affection too hardly they must not, I am
sure they will not be broken.   The mystic chords which pro-
ceeding from so many battle fields and so many patriot graves
pass through all the hearts and all the hearths in this broad
continent of ours will yet again harmonize in their ancient
music when breathed upon by the guardian angel of the nation."

(b) Lincoln's final version--

"I am loth to close. We are not enemies, but friends.
We must not be enemies.   Though passion may have strained,
it must not break our bonds of affection.   The mystic chords
of memory, stretching from every battle-field, and patriot
grave, to every living heart and hearthstone, all over this
broad land, will yet swell the chorus of the Union, when
again touched, as surely they will be, by the better angels
of our nature."

Since I can write almost as badly as Seward, I have no
hesitation in attaching some perorational ideas.

I trust you will prove as able a verbal alchemist as Lincoln.

Respectfully,

Philip L. Graham

Honorable John F. Kennedy
Washington, D. C.

17

KENNEDY'S CACOGRAPHY

Call it bad handwriting or poor penmanship—John F. Kennedy's cacography sometimes made it difficult for the unschooled to decipher what he had written.

"The thoughts flow too fast for the hand," was the sympathetic assessment of a handwriting analyst who studied the President's scrawl. His scribbles were, said the analyst, "evidently the writing of a very intelligent and cultured person. However, outside an inner circle of experienced readers, it seems more designed to mystify and impress than to communicate. It is in places much like shorthand, which is easily explainable when one considers the desire of the writer to master so many things well in a short space of time."

These notes, which JFK made in December 1960 while he was at his family's home in Palm Beach, reveal that one of the issues he was contemplating was outer space. (See the typed transcription below.) Kennedy would later challenge the country to send a man to the moon in a short space of time: before the decade was out. Apollo 11 commander Neil Armstrong took his celebrated small step onto the moon's surface on July 20, 1969.

1. Space

2. Disarmament
   • 100 people in
     govt
   • nuclear testing

3. China – Admission
   details on voting
   What about
   Taiwan - U.S.
         roles

4. Students and Voice of
   America

1. Space —

2. Disarmament
   Ⓐ 100 people
   ~~first~~
   Ⓑ nuclear testing

3. China — adversaries
   de Gaulson voting
   What about
   Taiwan — U.N.
   roles.

4. Students + vone
   America

JFK'S DICTATION OF HIS INAUGURAL ADDRESS

Evelyn Lincoln, Kennedy's secretary, was on board JKF's private plane *Caroline* when the President-elect flew to his family's home in Palm Beach, Florida, to prepare for his inaugural. This is when, on January 10th, ten days before the inauguration, Mrs. Lincoln took down in shorthand JFK's dictation for his inaugural address.

These pages from her steno pad include a reminder to herself to ask Mrs. Kennedy for the family Bible—this Mrs. Kennedy being Rose, JFK's mother. He used the family Bible for his swearing-in.

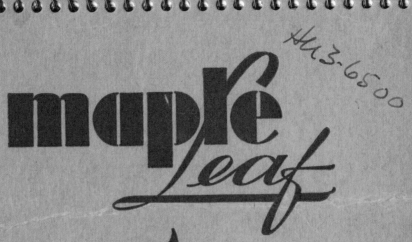

**STENOGRAPHIC
NOTE BOOK**

Ask for No. 16928T

NON-SLIP RUBBER EDGE

▼   ▼   ▼   ▼   ▼   ▼   ▼

1. Get birthday present for Elaine.

2. Get Bible from Mrs Kennedy for Chief Justice Warren.

3. Get in touch with Jerry Coleman & tell him to come to the apartment in N.Y. at 12:00 noon with some hats.

4. Case H Harkis.

5. Call Fred Erickson Re: Mrs Phillips Checks.

Write Fred Erickson to remove Dorothy Painter from payroll

Get Betty Burns Tel no.

Dictation on Inaugural
address enroute from
Washington to Palm
Beach —

descends

revaluts

- succes

5 —,

adams, Jeff

Mad

mmsve

35 (?)

3

como

republic.

legmatized

exp

Participate

concepts

etc

round

glob

sover
soverei sovereignty
sovereignty

etc

heritage

p 3, 4, 5,

page (separate)

exp

60's

voyage

circles

slide

friends

quick
sacrifice

a fate

twilight struggle

trumpet

battle

struggle

enemies

tyranny, poverty
disease
itself

force

enemies

alliance

events confidence

devotion

freedom

danger

world

involvement

[shorthand notes]

— sacrifice
— comradeship.

BACK-OF-THE-ENVELOPE ELOQUENCE

Among the imagery in the Inaugural Address is the trumpet, iconography inspired by a passage from the Bible on preparing for battle. Sorensen used the reverse side of a telegram from a U.S. Senator to jot down what became the final version of the "trumpet" sentence—illustrating how even the Office of the President-elect of the United States was not above the back-of-the-envelope capture of an idea.

JFK delivered the final iteration of the trumpet passage as it was written:

> "Now the trumpet summons us again—not as a call to bear arms, though arms we need—not as a call to battle, though embattled we are—but a call to bear the burden of a long twilight struggle, year in and year out, 'rejoicing in hope, patient in tribulation'—a struggle against the common enemies of man: tyranny, poverty, disease and war itself."

WESTERN UNION
TELEGRAM
W. P. MARSHALL, PRESIDENT

1201

The filing time shown in the date line on domestic telegrams is STANDARD TIME at point of origin. Time of receipt is STANDARD TIME at point of destination

UNQUOTE DETAILS COULD BE GIVEN CONGRESS LATER IN
SPECIAL MESSAGE. REST REGARDS=

1961 JAN 11 PM 6 31

ERNEST GRUENING USS=

(L) Now the trumpet summons us again — not as a call to arms, though arms we need — not as a call to battle, though embattled we are — but as a call to bear the burden of a long twilight struggle, year in and year out, rejoicing in hope, patient in tribulation — a struggle against the common enemies of man: tyranny, poverty, disease and war itself.

JFK'S HANDWRITTEN VERSION

The drafting of the thirty-fifth President's Inaugural Address employed the technology of the day—dictation, transcriptions, typewriters. But Kennedy wanted there to be a version in his own hand.

And so on January 17th, three days before the inauguration, on the flight from Palm Beach to Washington, D.C., JFK wrote out this draft of his Inaugural Address. The journalist Hugh Sidey, who was then a correspondent for *Time* magazine, was with JFK at the time.

January 17, 1961

The inaugural is a [beginning] an end
as well as a beginning. Today we are
[on 35th] [presence].
[Involved] on the all [of] the [?]
[?] [of] [when 3] [?]
the three [?] are with us today and
all those & those men who stood on
this same place, took the same
oath, made the same commitment.
to the [preservation] of this [American constitution] and
its [promise] [?] — [This is a disturbance]
that we have made today.
[world] [?] [?] on which we are

[we are a young people — but]
[an old Republic — but they] are
are old — at least as [for the life]
I [believe] [?] they are overcome,
we must [trust] [?] that we
[any] [?] we are descendants
[from] [?] — [?]

responsibility here on the last

And I believe freedom and freedom

The public we ... will understand that we have all done so in order to ... in order to win

the dissolution of the

defeat of the Revolutionary Communists
to which this country has always been
committed and which are now ...
expressed in the armed struggle.

The ... of which are our
ancestors fought here, we fight
around the globe. And we shall
pay any price, bear any burden,
meet any hardship, ...

... to

... of ... free ...
... and the freedom in the
to destroy wipe from the arms of her

49

Today we sound the trumpet
again, not a call to arms, though
arms we need— but a call to
battle, though embattled we are, but a
call a broader, more basic struggle
against the common enemies of man—
tyranny, poverty, disease, and
war itself.

Can we forge against these
enemies a grand alliance
north + south — east + west —
that can ensure a more fruitful life
for all men + women — Will you join in
this historic struggle. To few
generations has it been given
in the long history of the world — to here

chosen by events and will,
to be the chief defender of
freedom in a time of maximum
danger. I do not shrink from
this responsibility - I welcome it -
I do not believe any would change
places with any other people
or any other generation - the
the energy, faith, the devotion
and devotion to the cause of
freedom will lights this country
and those around the world
who stand on the best hope of
freedom. we lead on to take our
hands.

Do not

What your country is going to do
for you —   ask what you can do
for your country — my fellow
citizens of the world. ask not
                    or others
what America will do for you —
                        given you
but rather that you   can do
for freedom.   Nor of you —
the same high standards of
sacrifice and strength I have
and will ~~they~~ we seek from
you. ~~That~~ ~~alliances for~~
~~vice &~~ ~~progress~~ will be pursued

THE NEAR-FINAL VERSION

Kennedy and Sorensen continued to work on the speech in the days following JFK's dictation to Evelyn Lincoln.

This copy was typed on onionskin. The thin, somewhat brittle paper was once a ubiquitous item in offices, along with the carbon paper it was used with.

My Fellow-Citizens:

We ~~celebrate~~ *OBSERVE* today not a victory of party but a ~~convention~~ *CELEBRATION* of

freedom -- symbolizing an end as well as a beginning -- signifying renewal

as well as change. For I have sworn before you and Almighty God the same

solemn oath our forebears prescribed nearly a century and three-quarters ago.

The world is very different now, *FOR MAN HOLDS IN his* ~~empowered as it is to banish~~

MORTAL HANDS THE POWER *TO ABOLISH* all form of human poverty and *TO ABOLISH* all form of human life. And yet the same

revolutionary ~~concepts~~ *BELIEFS* for which ~~those~~ *OUR* forebears fought are still at issue

around the globe -- the ~~concept~~ *BELIEF* that the rights of man come not from the

generosity of the state but from the hand of God.

We dare not forget today that we are the heirs of that first

revolution. Let the word go forth from this time and place, to friend

and foe alike, that the torch ~~of liberty~~ has been passed to a new generation

of Americans -- born in this century, baptized by war, disciplined by a

cold and bitter peace, ~~but~~ proud of our ancient heritage -- and unwilling

to witness or permit the slow undoing of those ~~same concepts of~~ human

rights to which this nation has always been committed, and to which we

are committed today.

Let every nation know, whether it wish us well or ill, that we

shall pay any price, bear any burden, meet any hardship, support any friend

or oppose any foe in order to assure the survival and success of ~~freedom~~. *LIBERTY.*

This much we pledge -- and more.

To those old allies whose cultural and spiritual origins we share,

we pledge the loyalty of faithful friends. United, there is little we

61

COOPERATIVE

COPY

cannot do in a host of new ~~joint~~ ventures. Divided, there is little we

can do -- for we dare not meet a powerful ~~foe~~ CHALLENGE at odds and split asunder.

To those new states whom we now welcome to the ranks of the

free, we pledge our word that one form of colonial control shall not have

passed merely to be replaced by a far more iron tyranny. We shall not

~~always~~ expect to find ~~you on our side.~~ Them SUPPORTING OUR EVERY VIEW, But we shall always ~~expect~~ hope to find

~~you~~ Them vigorously ~~on the side of your~~ SUPPORTING THEIR own freedom of choice -- and ~~to~~ REMEMBER that, those

who foolishly ~~seek~~ SOUGHT TO FIND power by riding on the tiger's back inevitably ~~end~~ IN THE PAST,

ENDED up inside.

To those peoples in the huts and villages of half the globe

struggling to break the bonds of mass misery, we pledge our best efforts

to help ~~you~~ Them help ~~yourselves~~ Them selves, for whatever period is required -- not

because ~~the enemies~~ THE COMMUNISTS are doing it, not because we seek ~~your~~ Their votes, but

because it is right. If ~~freedom is way~~ THE FREE SOCIETY cannot help the many who are

poor, it can never save the few who are rich.

To our sister republics south of our border, WE OFFER a special pledge --

to convert ~~at last~~ our good words into good deeds -- in a new alliance

for progress -- to assist free men and free governments in casting off

the chains of poverty. But ~~your~~ THIS peaceful revolution of hope ~~must not~~ CANNOT

become the ~~tool~~ PREY of hostile powers. Let ~~every~~ ALL OUR neighbors know that we shall

join WITH THEM TO OPPOSE ~~to prevent~~ aggression or subversion anywhere in the Americas. And

let every other power know that this Hemisphere intends to remain master The

of its own house.

the UNITED NATIONS,

To that world assembly of sovereign states, ~~the last best hope~~

Do NoT CAPITALIZE COMMUNISTS

on ~~earth~~ -- ∧in an age where the instruments of war have far outpaced the instruments of peace -- we renew our pledge of support -- to ~~make it more than~~ merely prevent it becoming a forum for invective -- to strengthen its shield of the new and the weak -- and to enlarge the area to which its writ may run.

Finally, to those nations who would make themselves our ~~enemy~~ adversary, we offer not a pledge but a request: that both sides begin anew the quest for peace, before the dark powers of destruction unleashed by science engulf all humanity in planned or accidental self-destruction.

We dare not tempt ~~you~~ them with weakness. For only when our arms are sufficient beyond doubt can we be certain beyond doubt that they will never be employed.

But neither can two great and powerful ~~nations~~ groups of nations ~~long endure,~~ take comfort from their present ~~reckless~~ course, both sides overburdened by the ~~staggering~~ cost of modern weapons, both rightly alarmed by the steady spread of the deadly atom, yet both racing to alter that uncertain balance of terror that stays the hand of mankind's final war.

So let us begin anew -- remembering on both sides that civility is not a sign of weakness, and sincerity is always subject to proof. Let us never negotiate out of fear. But let us never fear to negotiate.

Let both sides explore what problems unite us instead of belaboring ~~what~~ the problems that divide us.

Let both sides, for the first time, formulate serious and precise proposals for the inspection and control of arms -- and bring the absolute power to destroy other nations under the absolute control of all nations.

4

COPY

Let both sides join to invoke the wonders of science instead of its terrors. Together let us explore the stars, conquer the deserts, eradicate disease, tap the ocean depths and encourage the arts and commerce.

Let both sides unite to heed in all corners of the earth the command of Isaiah -- to ~~loose the fetters of wickedness~~ . . . "undo the heavy burdens (and) . . . let the oppressed go free," . . . ~~deal thy bread to the hungry . . . bring the poor into thy house . . . (For) then shall thy light break forth as the morning . . .~~

And if a beach-head of cooperation can ~~push back~~ *be made in* the jungles of suspicion, let both sides join ~~someday in~~ *in the next task:* creating, not a new balance of power, but a new world of law, where the strong are just and the weak secure and the peace preserved forever. *where our children and their children can live out their lives without the ~~fear of~~ in opportunity and hope.*

All this will not be finished in the first one hundred days. Nor will it be finished in the first one thousand days, nor in the life of this Administration, nor even perhaps in our life-time on this planet. But let us begin.

In your hands, my fellow citizens, more than mine, will ~~rest~~ *in* *rest* ~~determined~~ the *final* success or failure of our course. Since this country was founded, each generation has been summoned to give testimony to its national loyalty. The graves of young Americans who answered that call encircle the globe.

Now the trumpet summons us again -- not as a call to bear arms, though arms we need -- not as a call to battle, though embattled we are -- but a call to bear the burden of a long twilight struggle, year in and year out, "rejoicing in hope, patient in tribulation" -- a struggle against

67

5

COPY

the common enemies of ~~man~~ MAN: tyranny, poverty, disease and war itself.

Can we forge against these enemies a grand and global alliance, North and South, East and West, that can assure a more fruitful life for all mankind? Will you join in that historic effort?

~~To few generations~~ In the long history of the world, ONLY A FEW GENERATIONS HAVE BEEN ~~have time and events~~ granted the role of ~~chief defenders of~~ defending freedom ~~at an~~ IN ITS hour of maximum danger. I do not shrink from this responsibility -- I welcome it ~~, when~~ I do not believe that any of us would exchange places with any other people or any other generation. The energy, the faith and the devotion which we bring to this endeavor will light our country and all who serve it -- and the glow from that fire can truly light the world. ~~For "when a man's ways please the Lord, he maketh even his enemies to be at peace with him."~~

And so, my fellow Americans: ask not what your country will do for you -- ask what you can do for your country.

My fellow citizens of the world: ask not what America will do for you, but what ~~you~~ TOGETHER WE can do for THE freedom OF MAN.

Finally, whether you are citizens of America or OF the world, ask of ~~us and those who serve with me~~ US the same high standards of strength and sacrifice that we ~~will~~ SHALL ask of you. ~~while asking the Lord above to grant us all the strength and wisdom we shall need.~~ With a good conscience our only sure reward, with history the final judge of our deeds, let us go forth to lead the land we love, asking His blessing and HIS help, but knowing that here on earth God's work must truly be our own.

KENNEDY AND CHURCHILL

Both John Kennedy and Winston Churchill were voracious readers, and both had concentrated periods in their adult lives when reading became pivotal to their careers. For Churchill, it was as an Army officer stationed in India in 1896. He was 22 and looking for ways to fill the empty hours. He read the books his father had read, absorbing Gibbon, Macaulay, Plato, Aristotle. For Kennedy, one such significant reading surge was in 1955, when the 38-year-old war hero was recovering from back surgery due to an injury he sustained while fighting in the Pacific. Among the writings he consumed were those by Winston Churchill.

Nor was that JFK's first exposure to Churchill. As the son of the United States' Ambassador to Great Britain, Kennedy was present in Parliament in 1939 when Churchill delivered his speech on Britain's duty to wage war against Hitler. As more than one historian has noted, Churchill's oratory had a profound effect on Kennedy.

It is not surprising, then, that the cadence of Churchill is at times the cadence of Kennedy. In JFK's "tyranny, poverty, disease and war itself" is heard the distant thunder of Churchill's "blood, toil, tears, and sweat."

Kennedy was also an inveterate note-taker, collecting quotes from personages in notebooks even while a student at Harvard. His notebook entries included biblical passages as well as those from such early orators as Cicero. Like Churchill, JFK had a precise memory and became his own font of *Bartlett's Familiar Quotations* (a book that Churchill memorized).

Churchill and Kennedy met only once, and briefly, on board Aristotle Onassis's yacht in the late 1950s. But their lives would intersect again in Kennedy's last year of life. On April 9th, 1963, with the aged Churchill's son and grandson appearing on Churchill's behalf, President Kennedy conferred on Winston Churchill the country's first honorary American citizenship.

THE INAUGURAL ADDRESS

…as it was delivered

The reading copy showing JFK's emendations

Kennedy Press Office
1737 L Street, N.W.
Washington, D. C.

N O T I C E

There should be no premature release
of this speech, nor should its contents
be paraphrased, alluded to or hinted at
in earlier stories. There is a total
embargo on this speech until 12 o'clock
Noon January 20, 1961, which includes
any and all references to any material
in the speech.

Pierre Salinger
Press Secretary

THE READING COPY

On the rostrum on Inauguration Day, in a plain black three-ring notebook, was the reading copy of the Inaugural Address that Kennedy referred to as he delivered his remarks. It consisted of 14 pages prepared on a large-print typewriter. (The phrase at the bottom of page 2 was an eleventh-hour addition that Sorensen suggested the day before the inauguration and Kennedy approved. This is why it appears in small capital letters: "AT HOME AND AROUND THE WORLD.")

The reading copy is devoid of cues to the speaker for where to pause or what to emphasize. But Kennedy had practiced—not only this speech (which he rehearsed even in the bath on the morning of his inauguration), but speechmaking in general. He had also listened with a speaker's ear to Churchill's delivery.

Like most great orators, JFK was not born one (nor was Churchill, who lisped), but he had been an able pupil of a voice coach. One of his corrections was to deliver his remarks more slowly, a technique Lincoln had also schooled himself in. (When Lincoln once asked a friend to deliver one of his speeches at a Republican rally he could not attend, his instructions to his friend were: "Read it slowly.")

The only marks Kennedy made on his reading copy were to add his signature and the date on the last page—these for posterity, as the pages were destined to be an historical document. He added these the day following the inauguration, so what was before him on January 20th was only what was to be spoken.

And yet, the reading copy would not be the final words that went forth starting at 12:51 p.m. Eastern Time on January 20, 1961: Kennedy changed some of the wording during his delivery.

On the pages that follow, the reader will see these changes, superimposed on the facsimiles. The changes are not, of course, part of the original document. But they serve to show the reader exactly where and how President John F. Kennedy was changing history even as he was making it.

In some areas he simplified imagery. In other places his changes, though subtle, created a stronger cadence through repetition of a word or phrase.

What is perhaps most surprising is that he changed his famous "ask not" sentence on the fly (page 101). With one simple change of word, a good sentence was transformed into a clarion call to action—the trumpet that to this day summons both JFK's memory and his mission. Such was Kennedy's genius as an orator.

~~My~~ Fellow-Citizens:

We observe today not a victory of party but a celebration of freedom-- symbolizing an end as well as a beginning -- signifying renewal as well as change. For I have sworn before you and Almighty God the same solemn oath our forebears prescribed nearly a century and three quarters ago.

The world is very different now. For man holds in his mortal hands the power to abolish all form_s of human poverty and ~~to abolish~~ all form_s of human life. And yet the same revolu- tionary beliefs for which our forebears fought are still at issue around the globe -- the belief that the rights of

man come not from the generosity of the state but from the hand of God.

We dare not forget today that we are the heirs of that first revolution. Let the word go forth from this time and place, to friend and foe alike, that the torch has been passed to a new generation of Americans -- born in this century, tempered by war, disciplined by a hard ~~cold~~ and bitter peace, proud of our ancient heritage -- and unwilling to witness or permit the slow undoing of those human rights to which this nation has always been committed, and to which we are committed today, AT HOME AND AROUND THE WORLD.

Let every nation know, whether

it wish_{es} us well or ill, that we shall
pay any price, bear any burden, meet
any hardship, support any friend, ~~or~~
oppose any foe ~~in order~~ to assure the
survival and the success of liberty.

This much we pledge -- and more.

To those old allies whose
cultural and spiritual origins we
share, we pledge the loyalty of
faithful friends. United, there is
little we cannot do in a host of ~~new~~
cooperative ventures. Divided, there
is little we can do -- for we dare
not meet a powerful challenge at odds
and split asunder.

To those new states whom we
~~now~~ welcome to the ranks of the free,

we pledge our word that one form of
colonial control shall not have passed ^{away}
merely to be replaced by a far more
iron tyranny. We shall not always
expect to find them supporting our
~~every~~ view. But we shall always hope
to find them strongly supporting their
own freedom -- and to remember that,
in the past, those who foolishly
sought ~~to find~~ power by riding ~~on~~
the _{back of the} tiger~~'s back inevitably~~ ended up
inside.

To those peoples in the huts
and villages of half the globe
struggling to break the bonds of mass
misery, we pledge our best efforts to
help them help themselves, for whatever

period is required -- not because the
communists ~~are~~ may be ^ doing it, not because
we seek their votes, but because it
is right. If ~~the~~ a free society cannot
help the many who are poor, it can ^ not
~~never~~ save the few who are rich.

To our sister republics south
of our border, we offer a special
pledge -- to convert our good words
into good deeds -- in a new alliance
for progress -- to assist free men
and free governments in casting off
the chains of poverty. But this
peaceful revolution of hope cannot
become the prey of hostile powers.
Let all our neighbors know that we
shall join with them to oppose

aggression or subversion anywhere in
the Americas. And let every other
power know that this Hemisphere intends
to remain the master of its own house.

To that world assembly of
sovereign states, the United Nations,
our last best hope in an age where
the instruments of war have far
outpaced the instruments of peace,
we renew our pledge of support --
to prevent ~~its~~ it from becoming merely a
forum for invective -- to strengthen
its shield of the new and the weak --
and to enlarge the area ~~to~~ in which
its writ may run.

Finally, to those nations who
would make themselves our adversary,

we offer not a pledge but a request:
that both sides begin anew the quest
for peace, before the dark powers of
destruction unleashed by science
engulf all humanity in planned or
accidental self-destruction.

We dare not tempt them with
weakness. For only when our arms are
sufficient beyond doubt can we be
certain beyond doubt that they will
never be employed.

But neither can two great and
powerful groups of nations take
comfort from ~~their~~ our present course --
both sides overburdened by the cost
of modern weapons, both rightly
alarmed by the steady spread of the

deadly atom, yet both racing to alter
that uncertain balance of terror that
stays the hand of mankind's final war.

So let us begin anew --
remembering on both sides that
civility is not a sign of weakness,
and sincerity is always subject to
proof. Let us never negotiate out
of fear. But let us never fear to
negotiate.

Let both sides explore what
problems unite us instead of belaboring
those   which
~~the~~ problems ~~that~~ divide us.

Let both sides, for the first
time, formulate serious and precise
proposals for the inspection and
control of arms -- and bring the

absolute power to destroy other nations
under the absolute control of all
nations.

Let both sides ~~join~~ seek to invoke
the wonders of science instead of its
terrors. Together let us explore
the stars, conquer the deserts,
eradicate disease, tap the ocean
depths and encourage the arts and
commerce.

Let both sides unite to heed
in all corners of the earth the
command of Isaiah -- to "undo the
heavy burdens . . . (and) let the
oppressed go free."

And if a beach-head of coopera-
tion ~~can be made in~~ may push back the jungles of

suspicion, let both sides join in
~~the next task:~~ creating, $\overset{\text{a new endeavor}}{\wedge}$ not a new
balance of power, but a new world of
law, where the strong are just and
the weak secure and the peace preserved.
~~forever~~.

      All this will not be finished
in the first one hundred days. Nor
will it be finished in the first one
thousand days, nor in the life of
this Administration, nor even perhaps
in our life-time on this planet.
But let us begin.

      In your hands, my fellow
citizens, more than ~~in~~ mine, will
rest the final success or failure of
our course. Since this country was

founded, each generation of Americans has been
summoned to give testimony to its
national loyalty. The graves of
young Americans who answered ~~that~~ the
call to service surround ~~encircle~~ the globe.

Now the trumpet summons us
again -- not as a call to bear arms,
though arms we need -- not as a call
to battle, though embattled we are --
but a call to bear the burden of a
long twilight struggle, year in and
year out, "rejoicing in hope, patient
in tribulation" -- a struggle against
the common enemies of man: tyranny,
poverty, disease and war itself.

Can we forge against these
enemies a grand and global alliance,

North and South, East and West, that
can assure a more fruitful life for
all mankind? Will you join in that
historic effort?

In the long history of the
world, only a few generations have
been granted the role of defending
freedom in its hour of maximum danger.
I do not shrink from this responsibility -- I welcome it. I do not
believe that any of us would exchange
places with any other people or any
other generation. The energy, the
faith, and the devotion which we bring
to this endeavor will light our
country and all who serve it -- and
the glow from that fire can truly

light the world.

And so, my fellow Americans:
ask not what your country ~~will~~ can do
for you -- ask what you can do for
your country.

My fellow citizens of the
world: ask not what America will
do for you, but what together we can
do for the freedom of man.

Finally, whether you are
citizens of America or ^citizens of the world,
ask of us ^here the same high standards of
strength and sacrifice ~~that~~ which we ~~shall~~
ask of you. With a good conscience
our only sure reward, with history
the final judge of our deeds, let us

go forth to lead the land we love,
asking His blessing and His help,
but knowing that here on earth God's
work must truly be our own.

John F. Kennedy

January 20th/1961

THE INAUGURAL ADDRESS

…as it lives in history

Roger G. Kennedy on the sacred fire of liberty

THE SACRED FIRE OF LIBERTY

"And so, my fellow Americans: ask not what your country can do for you—ask what you can do for your country. My fellow citizens of the world: ask not what America will do for you, but what together we can do for the freedom of man." President John F. Kennedy, Inaugural Address, January 1961

"There comes a time when a man has to take a stand and history will record that he has to meet these tough situations and ultimately make a decision." President John F. Kennedy to Secretary of Commerce Luther Hodges, June 1963

"Well, what the hell's the presidency for?" President Lyndon B. Johnson, November 1963

The summons

It is a masterpiece, the work of a man of first-rate intelligence, magnificently schooled, who had sought and received the aid of other craftsmen of language. But it is not the sheer art of John Fitzgerald Kennedy's Inaugural Address that moves us. Rather, it lives in our memories with our prayers, our favorite hymns and lines of poetry, because it is a summons we wish to heed, calling us and calling Kennedy himself to service beyond convenience or convention.

We do not merely admire that address—we are inspired by it. Other presidents had spoken eloquently to us. Kennedy spoke *for* us, and not only for those of us who were of his generation, though many of us feel a bond to him. He spoke for us all, of any age, as Americans, sharing across generational lines a commitment to freedom. He gave us a sense that we Americans have a special national history of sharing that commitment with all in the world who desire freedom. There have been bellicose and bullying perversions of that mission in our heritage as well, but Kennedy's invocation was to the generous spirit of those who created our nation and to those who have sustained it with the aid of our better angels.

The Inaugural Address is at its core a foreign-policy speech. Its power, however, comes from its transcending the necessities of the Cold War and its requiring more of us than we expect from exhortations to duty in any kind of war. Kennedy not only asked that we agree to defend our country; he summoned us as individuals to take up the cause of freedom in peace as we had in war, in a commitment that had neither boundaries nor time limits. Promising neither quick victories nor easy achievements, he invited us to "renew," to "begin anew," to rise once more to "a struggle against the common enemies of man: tyranny, poverty, disease and war itself."

"Now the trumpet summons us again," he said, not for a brief and glorious cavalry charge in the sunlight, but as "a call to bear the burden of a long twilight struggle, year in and year out, 'rejoicing in hope'" but also "'patient in tribulation,'" something most strange in the history of summonses. We were being asked not just to produce a spasm of heroic rectitude but to stand together in a sustained struggle—and more. We were to consider what we might ourselves do to advance the cause of freedom, not as agents of the nation, but as principals. He asked us to be colleagues in the covenant.

Kennedy's successor, Lyndon Johnson, put the term "covenant" as the title of his own Inaugural Address in 1965, reiterating the compact among the people and their president: "The American covenant [has] called on us to help show the way for the liberation of man." This was not a biblical covenant granted to a chosen people by the Almighty, nor a written *ex parte* declaration, like the covenant to a will. It was instead a grand mutual assent to shared responsibility, in the tradition of the Mayflower Compact and the Declaration of Independence—a tradition to which Franklin Roosevelt, the paradigm for both Johnson and Kennedy, called the nation in his own Third Inaugural Address.

> **W**e were being asked not just to produce a spasm of heroic rectitude but to stand together in a sustained struggle.

Even now, after nearly a half-century of disappointments, including some arising from Kennedy's own deficiencies and many from our own, Kennedy's summons to an affirming partnership thrills us as it did when we first heard it. His cadences have lost no vitality; they still call us toward a common endeavor for our country, and also for "those human rights to which this nation has always been committed, and to which we are committed today, at home and around the world." Kennedy opened his arms to us as his partners, and as a good partner does, he told us what we needed to know: we could not be sure of the limits of our obligations, in geography or in time, nor could we be content to await directives as to what we might be obligated to do.

In Roosevelt's time it would have been politically perilous to include "fellow citizens of the world" in an American covenant; Roosevelt would not have used that phrase in 1936. Even three years later, when the world went back to war, voices were still raised in the United States Senate deriding "One Worlders." But in 1941 the Japanese attacked Pearl Harbor, and they and their European allies declared themselves America's enemies. The Cold War and the nuclear arms race followed. The torches passed from one generation to the next lit a new reality.

When Kennedy spoke, it had become true that "man holds in his mortal hands the power to abolish all forms of human poverty and all forms of human life." Yet that did not wipe clear the obligation felt by many Americans, given eloquent restatement by Kennedy, that despite the terrors of nuclear war, "the same revolutionary beliefs for which our forebears fought…[were] still at issue around the globe." Recalling the phrase "the sacred fire of liberty" that both George Washington and Franklin Roosevelt used, Kennedy asked of us that we, too, find "[t]he energy, the faith, the devotion" not just to "light our country," but also to provide a "glow from that fire…[to] truly light the world."

The magic of Kennedy's summons lay in his treating us as partners, and not just as willing foot soldiers, and in his invitation to join with him in keeping alight "that fire" around the world in peaceful ways.

What a change had come over our country in the forty years since President Warren Harding's Inaugural Address. In the distant time beyond worldwide depression and a second worldwide war, Harding had celebrated an "inherited policy of noninvolvement in Old World affairs….Confident of our ability to work out our own destiny, and jealously guarding our right to do so, we seek no part in directing the destinies of the Old World. We do not mean to be entangled. We will accept no responsibility except as our own conscience and judgment, in each instance, may determine…. America…can be a party to no permanent military alliance. It can enter into no political commitments, nor assume any economic obligations which will subject our decisions to any other than our own authority…[with] nationality exalted….This is not selfishness, it is sanctity. It is not aloofness, it is security. It is not suspicion of others, it is patriotic adherence to the things which made us what we are."

Kennedy did not need to respond to Harding. The attack on Pearl Harbor had done that, and by 1945 we all had in mind "[t]he graves of young Americans who answered the call to service…[that surrounded] the globe." Kennedy also echoed in his own speech the answer to Harding that Roosevelt had given in his wartime Fourth Inaugural Address when he said: "We have learned that we cannot live alone, at peace; that our own well-being is dependent on the well-being of other nations far away. We have learned that we must live as men, not as ostriches, nor as dogs in the manger….We have learned to be citizens of the world, members of the human community."

> He was asking a peacetime commitment to the cause of freedom from people who might otherwise sink into post-war cynicism and selfishness.

In 1961 Kennedy had to rekindle that spirit if he were to recruit volunteers from a generation of which much had already been required, in declared war and in the Cold War. He was asking a peacetime commitment to the cause of freedom from people who might otherwise sink into post-war cynicism and selfishness. Yet Kennedy took up the trumpet and blew the call. To service! Once more! He expected us—and he expected himself—to summon again the urgent energy of wartime.

The voice and accent were John Kennedy's, but the cadences were Winston Churchill's on that inaugural day. It was as if Kennedy's voice faded into Churchill's, crackling through speakers in barracks and on radios in living rooms. Both seemed to be saying to us and the world: "we shall pay any price, bear any burden, meet any hardship, support any friend, oppose any foe to assure the survival and the success of liberty."

Did we not hear other voices as well? In his Third Inaugural Address, Franklin Roosevelt had invoked George Washington. "The destiny of America was proclaimed in words of prophecy...by our first President in his first inaugural in 1789...: 'The preservation of the sacred fire of liberty and the destiny of the republican model of government are...staked on the experiment entrusted to the hands of the American people.'...If we lose that sacred fire...then we shall reject the destiny which Washington strove so valiantly and so triumphantly to establish." In his Fourth Inaugural Address, in 1945, Roosevelt pledged "the people of the Republic" to keep alight that "sacred fire of liberty" around the war-ravaged world, as Eisenhower in his Second Inaugural Address in 1957 had invoked "the light of freedom, coming to all darkened lands, [to] flame brightly—until at last the darkness is no more."

Kennedy's Inaugural Address included both admissions of inheritance and assertions of coming of age.

Eisenhower had sustained Roosevelt's internationalism into Kennedy's time, proclaiming in his First Inaugural Address that "the strength of all free peoples lies in unity; their danger, in discord....[Believing] the defense of freedom, like freedom itself, to be one and indivisible, we hold all continents and peoples in equal regard and honor. We reject any insinuation that one race or another, one people or another, is in any sense inferior or expendable." And then, presaging Kennedy's "ask not," Eisenhower told the nation: "It is the firm duty of each of our free citizens and of every free citizen everywhere to place the cause of his country before the comfort, the convenience of himself."

In his Second Inaugural Address, he reiterated his repudiation of Harding's smugness: "...one truth must rule all we think and all we do. No people can live to itself alone. The unity of all who dwell in freedom is their only sure defense. The economic need of all nations—in mutual dependence—makes isolation an impossibility; not even America's prosperity could long survive if other nations did not also prosper. No nation can longer be a fortress, lone and strong and safe. And any people, seeking such shelter for themselves, can now build only their own prison."

A renewed covenant for a new generation

John Fitzgerald Kennedy came to the presidency at the age of 43, the youngest man ever to be elected to the office. (Theodore Roosevelt was a year younger when he took office, having been elected as Vice President to William McKinley, who was assassinated.) Kennedy was succeeding Eisenhower, the national patriarch who had led the armies of his own nation and its allies in a victorious war. Eisenhower was 70 as he sat on the platform listening to his successor, who had never risen above the rank of lieutenant.

Kennedy's Inaugural Address included both admissions of inheritance and assertions of coming of age. He stood in a tradition, but he stood on his own feet. His debts to Franklin Roosevelt were more than rhetorical; the very presidency he was commencing was a different one than that which came to Roosevelt in 1932. Kennedy brought his own magic, but Roosevelt had beckoned him onward to use it. No wonder he said:

"We dare not forget today that we are…heirs….Let the word go forth…that the torch has been passed to a new generation of Americans—born in this century, tempered by war, disciplined by a hard and bitter peace, proud of our ancient heritage…." Kennedy spoke as the leader of that "new generation," offering pledges in its name, and calling to mind Roosevelt's declaration of his representative role for the preceding generation. Many people who heard Kennedy in 1961 had heard Roosevelt assert in 1936, when accepting the presidential nomination for the second time, that "[t]here is a mysterious cycle in human events. To some generations, much is given. Of other generations, much is expected. This generation of Americans has a rendezvous with destiny."

Kennedy did not use Roosevelt's expression, although he told his inaugural audience that "[i]n the long history of the world, only a few generations have been granted the role of defending freedom in its hour of maximum danger. I do not shrink from this responsibility—I welcome it. I do not believe that any of us would exchange places with any other people or any other generation."

In his "rendezvous with destiny" speech in 1936, Roosevelt renewed the compact made in his Chicago acceptance speech in 1932: "I pledge you, I pledge myself, to a new deal for the American people." So important was that pledge that the term "new deal" interposed between leader and people was neither capitalized in the text nor emphasized in the delivery. What mattered was the nominee's assurance of his

> When inaugurating their presidencies, Roosevelt and Kennedy no longer spoke only for themselves.

readiness to be in the front rank of the generation's mutual commitments. When inaugurating their presidencies, Roosevelt and Kennedy no longer spoke only for themselves; they became representative. Thereafter instinct, as well as rhetorical calculation, led them to substitute "we" for "I" in their pledges.

Roosevelt's transition from individual to leader of a nation came as he asserted his "firm belief that the only thing we have to fear is fear itself," placing upon his shoulders the tremendous historic burden of being tested by the standards of Washington and Lincoln. "In every dark hour of our national life," he said, "a leadership of frankness and vigor" had emerged, and in offering to give that kind of leadership, he sought a reciprocal commitment from the nation to be served: "these dark days will be worth all they cost us," Roosevelt said, "if they teach us that our true destiny is not to be ministered unto but to

111

minister to ourselves and to our fellow men." *Ask not*, he might have said next. Instead he spoke more philosophically of that "interdependence" that the Reverend Martin Luther King Jr. would describe in 1968 as "an inescapable network of mutuality, tied in a single garment of destiny on each other."

"We can not merely take," said Roosevelt, "but we must give as well…willing to sacrifice for the good of a common discipline.…"

In 1937, in his Second Inaugural Address, Roosevelt asserted the covenanting parties to be "We of the Republic," evoking the phrase "We the People of the United States," contributed by Gouverneur Morris to the Preamble to the Constitution. As Lincoln observed in 1860, Morris's formulation asserted that it was the people, not the states, that came together to form the covenanting nation. And as Roosevelt commented: "Our covenant with ourselves did not stop there. Instinctively we recognized a deeper need—the need to find through government the instrument of our united purpose to solve for the individual the ever-rising problems of a complex civilization."

> As Lincoln observed, it was the people, not the states, that came together to form the covenanting nation.

In his Third Inaugural Address, in 1941, Roosevelt returned to the theme of the American covenant, for the first time placing it within an international setting and a longer story. "In the Americas its impact has been irresistible…not because this continent was a new-found land, but because all those who came here believed they could create upon this continent a new life—a life that should be new in freedom. Its vitality was written into our own Mayflower Compact, into the Declaration of Independence, into the Constitution of the United States, into the Gettysburg Address…[gaining] stature and clarity with each generation."

In 1620 the Mayflower Compact had united "mutually" a band of Pilgrims, scarred and weary of civil strife. As if putting their weapons on the table, they conceded to a new "body politic" their individual access to violence. Promising "all due submission and obedience" they did "covenant and combine…to enact, constitute, and frame, such just and equal laws, ordinances, acts, constitutions and offices, from time to time, as shall be thought most meet and convenient for the general good."

Their compact established an American propensity for writing down important agreements, which thereafter produced many laws and ordinances, as well as a written Declaration of Independence and a written Constitution. In the Declaration, the Founding Fathers boldly agreed to establish a much larger "body politick," dedicated to the propositions that "all men are created equal; that they are endowed by their Creator with certain unalienable rights; that among these are life, liberty, and the pursuit of happiness." Their revolutionary covenant gave birth to a new kind of government, "deriving…[its] just powers from the consent of the governed…[i]n the name and by the authority of the good people of these colonies." The signers described themselves as "representatives of the United States of America…mutually…[pledging] to each other our lives, our fortunes, and our sacred honor."

Ratified in 1788, the Constitution followed a seven-year war and a four-year failed effort thereafter to manage an inchoate Confederation, often disrupted by racial and class violence. The contracting parties were "the people of the United States," who by then had every reason to desire "a more perfect union" and to "insure domestic tranquility."

Their fragile and partial Constitutional compact broke apart in 1861. The founding principles to which it had been explicitly "dedicated" had been eaten away by the corrosion of race-based slavery. Abraham Lincoln's Gettysburg Address was delivered in a place where it was impossible to avoid the terrible truth of failure: he spoke to consecrate a burial ground, when the graves were still fresh. At Gettysburg two armies of related people had suffered more than 50,000 casualties in three days of mutual maiming and killing.

As Commander in Chief, Lincoln reconsecrated the covenant to a "new birth of freedom." Then, in his Second Inaugural Address, on March 4, 1865, he asked that his countrymen join him in that rededication, acknowledging the tragic history of the national covenant and its unfulfilled requirements. We often hear Lincoln's words of consolation, "with malice toward none, with charity for all." They are more familiar because they are easier to accept than his words of remonstrance and exhortation: "with firmness in the right, let us strive to finish the work we are in." That work was being done on the battlefields and also in the legislatures, finishing the tasks left unfulfilled by the delinquencies of the intervening generations. Finishing that work did indeed require a "new birth of freedom"—a full reaffirmation of the principles of the covenant. Yet

> **Lincoln's Gettysburg Address was delivered in a place where it was impossible to avoid the terrible truth of failure.**

another "new birth"—for yet another generation—was required in the civil rights acts of the 1960s, and the work is never fully finished. Despite the works of redemption of the year of miracles, 2008, there is much yet to be done. "Let us strive to finish the work we are in"—those are still the operable words for us.

Lincoln's imperatives energized John Kennedy's summons to "ask what you can do for your country." The answer required of those who knew their history, and honored it, was that we were—and are—called to finish the work of Lincoln.

113

What Kennedy asked of himself

Kennedy's Inaugural Address stirs us as it does because it invites us to take up our obligations under the American covenant, to act for the common good—with our President entering the covenant with us. We know from John Kennedy's subsequent actions that he was summoning himself as he summoned us. We had work to do; so had he. He did not end his speech with the famous summons. He went on to invite his listeners to include him among the participants in the continuing compact. He looked out to the crowd and beyond it to the nation, and urged his generation to "ask of us…the same high standards of strength and sacrifice which we ask of you. With a good conscience our only sure reward, with history the final judge of our deeds, let us go forth to lead the land we love, asking His blessing and His help, but knowing that here on earth God's work must truly be our own."

Kennedy's Inaugural Address moves us for a further reason. Its covenant was a capacious one, grounded in a broad public morality we now read into it from Kennedy's "Report to the American People on Civil Rights" of June 11, 1963, which was, in truth, his second inaugural address. Taking the two together, we now understand how important it was for him in 1963 to include within the compact the obligations and opportunities of his generation at home as well as abroad to which he had summoned us in 1961. We were to join together in service to "those human rights to which this nation has always been committed, and to which we are committed today, at home and around the world."

Kennedy's "Report on Civil Rights" of June 11, 1963 was, in truth, his second inaugural address.

On the great question of civil rights, there was not one syllable in Kennedy's Inaugural Address. He began to fill in that omission in his Report on Civil Rights, bringing the "sacred fire" home again to light up the dark corners of the American experiment. As Franklin Roosevelt admonished his countrymen, the highest aspirations of that experiment had been "entrusted to the hands of the American people"—and remained shadowed. As Kennedy said in his Inaugural Address, and might say today, "[t]he energy, the faith, the devotion which we bring to this endeavor will light our country and all who serve it—and the glow from that fire can truly light the world." The most telling four minutes in Kennedy's Report, recalling both Washington and Roosevelt, were not scripted. They came at the end, spoken from the heart. That is why we can perhaps feel them more profoundly in our hearts than we do many of the magnificent phrases in the Inaugural Address.

In those final four minutes, Kennedy stated that the "moral issue" at the core of the nation's life during his presidency was "as old as the scriptures and…as clear as the American Constitution….The heart of the question is whether all Americans are afforded equal rights and equal opportunities, whether we are going to treat our fellow Americans as we want to be treated."

The Inaugural Address itself becomes what we wish to remember because we can complete it, as he did, with his Report on Civil Rights and the actions of his final months in office. The Address was, as he said, "both an end and a beginning." We know now what lay ahead of him when he said, "we shall pay any price...to assure the survival and the success of liberty," and went on to say, "This much we pledge—and more."

That "more" came later, in his Report on Civil Rights, calling his generation to *its* rendezvous with destiny. His Inaugural Address now comes to our ears together with its completion in that later speech. Together they tell us that throughout his presidency he was growing into greatness.

The end and the beginning

Kennedy's term in office was, as he said, "the end" of a long and tortured national history in which the relationship of the American covenant to slavery and its after-effects was so integral as to be discussed in more than half the presidential inaugural addresses, beginning in the 1830s. Those previous inaugural addresses had been testimony to the twistings and turnings of

> His Inaugural Address was a beginning of a course of redemption.

national policy, and some presidents, beginning with Martin Van Buren in 1837, had actually used inaugural occasions to twist it further. Kennedy took office after his own erratic and ambiguous history with civil rights; it was not at all certain how this privileged and glamorous young man would respond to a test of his commitment to equal rights, under a full covenant, for all the people.

After half his elected term in office had passed in further ambiguity, Kennedy rose to that test in the final year of his presidency. Because he did not live to complete his achievement, his Inaugural Address was close to its conclusion. It was also, however, a beginning of a course of redemption, not just for himself but also for his generation and his country. He was killed in mid-response to his own summons, leaving his successor, Lyndon B. Johnson, to carry on.

Kennedy and Johnson together renewed the covenant to the full meaning for all citizens stated in the inaugural addresses of Abraham Lincoln and the seven presidents who succeeded him. They had to compensate for the silence or inaction of six presidents thereafter, but building upon the efforts of their three immediate predecessors, they restored the Lincolnian covenant to an amplitude that included all Americans, and by implication, all people who would wish to live in freedom, on their own terms within their own covenants.

The first stage in the testing of Kennedy's serious intent lay in the degree to which he would act upon the last-minute insertion of two words in his Inaugural Address—"at home": two words with immense implications. With them in place, the sentence represented a commitment to "those human rights to

115

which this nation has always been committed, and to which we are committed today, at home and around the world."

The inclusion of those words mattered a great deal to those denied those rights at home, as well as to those who regarded the systematic denial of those rights as the greatest problem confronting the nation at home. Among those to whom they mattered were Father Theodore Hesburgh, then the president of the University of Notre Dame, and two members of Kennedy's inner circle, Harris Wofford and Lewis Martin. Father Hesburgh told Kennedy through Wofford that failure to use the government's full powers to end racial discrimination was "the central moral problem of our times." And the Pulitzer Prize-winning journalist Nick Kotz wrote that the issue of civil rights was "beyond question, the most critical…facing the country."

The Reverend King and other leaders of Black America were in the streets. White allies were marching with them and organizing protests, while sheriffs in the South were using attack dogs and fire hoses against them. And two words—"at home"— were all that went into the Inaugural Address about civil rights, and they only after intense and vehement insistence by Wofford and Martin. It must be said, though it is painful to say it: the Inaugural Address follows an Inaugural Oath. The Oath includes a pledge to enforce the Constitution. And the Constitution includes the Civil Rights Amendments— the 13th, 14th, and 15th.

Kennedy was opening the compact toward a full covenant for "all our citizens."

A year of equivocation limped by, as Kennedy appointed segregationist judges and his brother Robert, the Attorney General, discouraged civil rights protests. Wofford and Martin kept trying, though they did not succeed in inserting even two words about civil rights in Kennedy's report of May 25, 1961, "Special Message to the Congress on Urgent National Needs." After years of racial violence and ten days of racial rioting in Alabama, nearly all the urgencies listed were related to the defense budget— not civil rights. Father Hesburgh listened to the speech with Wofford and afterward exploded: "I don't care if the United States gets the first man on the moon if we dawdle along here on our corner of the earth, nursing our prejudices, flouting our magnificent Constitution…and appearing hypocrites to the world."

The true beginning came soon thereafter. In June 1963 Kennedy told his Commerce Secretary, Luther Hodges, that "[t]here comes a time when a man has to take a stand and history will record that he has to meet these tough situations and ultimately make a decision." Later in that month, he delivered his Report on Civil Rights on radio and television, confident in tone, uncompromising in its implications, essentially as an expansion of the two crucial words "at home"—filling out what had been missing from his Inaugural Address. The first Roman Catholic to be elected President of the United States took up Father Hesburgh's "moral issue" as a "tough situation" that he was himself summoned to meet, for his country and for all those aspiring to freedom, and in his great summation of the lessons of scripture and experience, he reminded his countrymen that "the heart of the question" was "whether all Americans are to be afforded equal rights and equal opportunities, whether we are going to treat our fellow Americans as we want to be treated. If an American, because his skin is dark, cannot eat lunch in a restaurant open to the public, if he cannot send his children to the best public school available, if he cannot vote for the public officials who represent him, if, in short, he cannot enjoy the full and free life which all of us want, then who among us would be content to have the color of his skin changed and stand in his place? Who among us would then be content with the counsels of patience and delay? One hundred years of delay have passed since President Lincoln freed the slaves, yet their heirs, their grandsons, are not fully free. They are not yet freed from the bonds of injustice. They are not yet freed from social and economic oppression. And this nation, for all its hopes and all its boasts, will not be fully free until all its citizens are free….This is a matter which concerns this country and what it stands for, and in meeting it I ask the support of all our citizens."

Kennedy was opening the compact toward a full covenant for "all our citizens." He announced that he was placing before the Congress what became the Civil Rights Act of 1964, and he went to Dallas and to his death a few months later with a prepared statement of the imperatives for that legislation.

During the week after Kennedy's assassination, Lyndon Johnson was counseled by the leaders of his party not to press ahead with the Civil Rights Act. At a meeting in his living room in the Washington suburb of Spring Valley, before moving into the White House, Johnson listened to their counsels of prudence and further dawdling, and responded with words fit for a bronze monument on the White House grounds: "Well, what the hell's the presidency for?"

Thereafter, Johnson developed a working alliance with King and the Freedom Riders, cross-ruffing between action on the streets and action in the corridors of Congress, while they both began speaking explicitly of the full covenant. It became the centerpiece of Johnson's own Inaugural Address, binding the nation. "Justice requires us to remember that when any citizen denies his fellow, saying, 'His color is not mine'…in that moment he betrays America, though his

By the end of 1963, a politician prone to calculation was rising beyond calculation to commitment.

forebears created this Nation. Men want to be a part of a common enterprise—a cause greater than themselves. Each of us must find a way to advance the purpose of the Nation, thus finding new purpose for ourselves. Without this, we shall become a nation of strangers."

At the National Cathedral, on March 31, 1968, King issued his own summons to heed the requirements of the covenant: "[A]ll life is inter-related. All persons are caught in an inescapable network of mutuality, tied in a single garment of destiny. Whatever affects one directly affects all indirectly. I can never be what I ought to be until you are what you ought to be. And you can never be what you ought to be until I am what I ought to be. This is the inter-related structure of reality."

The work is not yet done. On January 20, 2009 we gave ourselves a fresh beginning, justifying the pride and rejoicing we felt when we first heard President Kennedy's Inaugural Address. Kennedy, King, Johnson, and those who worked with them brought us to this place. And Kennedy's sense of the tradition in which he took his place on that cold day in January 1961 situated him, and us, within a continuing chronicle of which we may be proud to have a part. An accommodating man who had always sought to avoid confrontation was confronted with a "tough situation." Over the next two years, he responded with hope rather than fear, with action rather than acquiescence. By the end of 1963, a politician prone to calculation was rising beyond calculation to commitment. A cautious candidate was committing his full faith, credit, life, political capital and sacred honor to a full covenant.

The Inaugural Address was Kennedy's most polished performance and remains his most famous utterance. It was not, however, the high point of his political life. He rose to that in the final months of 1963, and of his life.

Jo Callan from the Press Office –

They have had a query as to source of the following quote from

the President's Inaugural Address "rejoicing in hope, patient in

tribulation"

1/27/61
5:00

EPILOGUE

Transcription of the Recorded Speech

Vice President Johnson, Mr. Speaker, Mr. Chief Justice, President Eisenhower, Vice President Nixon, President Truman, Reverend Clergy, fellow citizens:

We observe today not a victory of party but a celebration of freedom—symbolizing an end as well as a beginning—signifying renewal as well as change. For I have sworn before you and Almighty God the same solemn oath our forbears prescribed nearly a century and three-quarters ago.

The world is very different now. For man holds in his mortal hands the power to abolish all forms of human poverty and all forms of human life. And yet the same revolutionary beliefs for which our forebears fought are still at issue around the globe—the belief that the rights of man come not from the generosity of the state but from the hand of God.

We dare not forget today that we are the heirs of that first revolution. Let the word go forth from this time and place, to friend and foe alike, that the torch has been passed to a new generation of Americans—born in this century, tempered by war, disciplined by a hard and bitter peace, proud of our ancient heritage—and unwilling to witness or permit the slow undoing of those human rights to which this nation has always been committed, and to which we are committed today, at home and around the world.

Let every nation know, whether it wishes us well or ill, that we shall pay any price, bear any burden, meet any hardship, support any friend, oppose any foe to assure the survival and the success of liberty.

This much we pledge—and more.

To those old allies whose cultural and spiritual origins we share, we pledge the loyalty of faithful friends. United, there is little we cannot do in a host of cooperative ventures. Divided, there is little we can do—for we dare not meet a powerful challenge at odds and split asunder.

To those new states whom we welcome to the ranks of the free, we pledge our word that one form of colonial control shall not have passed away merely to be replaced by a far more iron tyranny. We shall not always expect to find them supporting our view. But we shall always hope to find them strongly supporting their own freedom—and to remember that, in the past, those who foolishly sought power by riding the back of the tiger ended up inside.

To those people in the huts and villages of half the globe struggling to break the bonds of mass misery, we pledge our best efforts to help them help themselves, for whatever period is required—not because the communists may be doing it, not because we seek their votes, but because it is right. If a free society cannot help the many who are poor, it cannot save the few who are rich.

To our sister republics south of our border, we offer a special pledge—to convert our good words into good deeds—in a new alliance for progress—to assist free men and free governments in casting off the chains of poverty. But this peaceful revolution of hope cannot become the prey of hostile powers. Let all our neighbors know that we shall join with them to oppose aggression or subversion anywhere in the Americas. And let every other power know that this Hemisphere intends to remain the master of its own house.

To that world assembly of sovereign states, the United Nations, our last best hope in an age where the instruments of war have far outpaced the instruments of peace, we renew our pledge of support—to prevent it from becoming merely a forum for invective—to strengthen its shield of the new and the weak—and to enlarge the area in which its writ may run.

Finally, to those nations who would make themselves our adversary, we offer not a pledge but a request: that both sides begin anew the quest for peace, before the dark powers of destruction unleashed by science engulf all humanity in planned or accidental self-destruction.

We dare not tempt them with weakness. For only when our arms are sufficient beyond doubt can we be certain beyond doubt that they will never be employed.

But neither can two great and powerful groups of nations take comfort from our present course—both sides overburdened by the cost of modern weapons, both rightly alarmed by the steady spread of the deadly atom, yet both racing to alter that uncertain balance of terror that stays the hand of mankind's final war.

So let us begin anew—remembering on both sides that civility is not a sign of weakness, and sincerity is always subject to proof. Let us never negotiate out of fear. But let us never fear to negotiate.

Let both sides explore what problems unite us instead of belaboring those problems which divide us.

Let both sides, for the first time, formulate serious and precise proposals for the inspection and control of arms—and bring the absolute power to destroy other nations under the absolute control of all nations.

Let both sides seek to invoke the wonders of science instead of its terrors. Together let us explore the stars, conquer the deserts, eradicate disease, tap the ocean depths and encourage the arts and commerce.

Let both sides unite to heed in all corners of the earth the command of Isaiah—to "undo the heavy burdens...(and) let the oppressed go free."

And if a beach-head of cooperation may push back the jungle of suspicion, let both sides join in creating a new endeavor, not a new balance of power, but a new world of law, where the strong are just and the weak secure and the peace preserved.

All this will not be finished in the first one hundred days. Nor will it be finished in the first one thousand days, nor in the life of this Administration, nor even perhaps in our life-time on this planet. But let us begin.

In your hands, my fellow citizens, more than mine, will rest the final success or failure of our course. Since this country was founded, each generation of Americans has been summoned to give testimony to its national loyalty. The graves of young Americans who answered the call to service surround the globe.

Now the trumpet summons us again—not as a call to bear arms, though arms we need—not as a call to battle, though embattled we are—but a call to bear the burden of a long twilight struggle, year in and year out, "rejoicing in hope, patient in tribulation"—a struggle against the common enemies of man: tyranny, poverty, disease and war itself.

Can we forge against these enemies a grand and global alliance, North and South, East and West, that can assure a more fruitful life for all mankind? Will you join in that historic effort?

In the long history of the world, only a few generations have been granted the role of defending freedom in its hour of maximum danger. I do not shrink from this responsibility—I welcome it. I do not believe that any of us would exchange places with any other people or any other generation. The energy, the faith, the devotion which we bring to this endeavor will light our country and all who serve it—and the glow from that fire can truly light the world.

And so, my fellow Americans: ask not what your country can do for you—ask what you can do for your country.

My fellow citizens of the world: ask not what America will do for you, but what together we can do for the freedom of man.

Finally, whether you are citizens of America or citizens of the world, ask of us here the same high standards of strength and sacrifice which we ask of you. With a good conscience our only sure reward, with history the final judge of our deeds, let us go forth to lead the land we love, asking His blessing and His help, but knowing that here on earth God's work must truly be our own.

SOURCES AND RECOMMENDATIONS

The commentary

There are hundreds of excellent books on the presidencies of John F. Kennedy and Lyndon Johnson; an appreciative bibliography would be larger than this book. The two from which Roger Kennedy recounted key conversations are *The Bystander: John F. Kennedy and the Struggle for Black Equality* by Nick Bryant (Basic Books, 2006), and *Judgment Days: Lyndon Baines Johnson, Martin Luther King, Jr., and the Laws That Changed America* by Nick Kotz (Houghton Mifflin, 2005). Both provide extensive bibliographies dealing with the period.

Mr. Kennedy supplemented these written accounts with renewed conversations—and recollections of past conversations—with many of the principal figures of the time, among them Berl Bernhard, Warren E. Burger, Eugene McCarthy, Harry McPherson, Arthur Schlesinger Jr., James W. Symington, Harris Wofford, and John Zentay.

The facsimiles

All facsimiles of documents are from the archives of the John F. Kennedy Presidential Library and Museum. They have been reproduced in their actual size, with the exceptions of JFK's handwritten version of his Inaugural Address and Sorensen's handwritten notes on the word counts of other inaugural addresses. Both of these were written on legal-size paper.

We consulted three works by Theodore Sorensen: *Kennedy* (Harper & Row, 1965), *"Let the Word Go Forth": The Speeches, Statements, and Writings of John F. Kennedy, 1947 to 1963* (Dell, 1988), and *Counselor: A Life at the Edge of History* (Harper, 2008).

Two invaluable sources on JFK's Inaugural Address are *Ask Not: The Inauguration of John F. Kennedy and the Speech That Changed America* by Thurston Clarke (Henry Holt, 2004) and *Sounding the Trumpet: The Making of John F. Kennedy's Inaugural Address* by Richard J. Tofel (Ivan R. Dee, 2005). We also recommend *Live from the Campaign Trail: The Greatest Presidential Campaign Speeches of the Twentieth Century and How They Shaped Modern America* by Michael Cohen (Walker & Company, 2008).

For the discussion on JFK and Lincoln, we referenced *The Eloquent President: A Portrait of Lincoln Through His Own Words* by Ronald C. White Jr. (Random House, 2005). We recommend his *A. Lincoln: A Biography* (Random House, 2009).

For the discussion on JFK and Winston Churchill, our sources were "The Statesman John Kennedy Most Admired" by Fred Glueckstein (in *Finest Hour: Journal of The Churchill Centre, no. 129, Winter*

2005-06) and numerous works by Richard M. Langworth, in particular his *Churchill by Himself: The Definitive Collection of Quotations* (Public Affairs, 2008).

The experience

Finally, we encourage all students and admirers of JFK to visit his Presidential Library outside Boston. Start with a virtual tour, at www.jfklibrary.org, but do experience the dramatic I. M. Pei building at Columbia Point if the opportunity arises.

Gazing out of its soaring windows to the surrounding Boston waterfront may inspire one to summon the laudatory words of E. B. White, writing of John F. Kennedy eight days after November 22, 1963:

"It can be said of him…that he did not fear the weather, and did not trim his sails, but instead challenged the wind itself."

ABOUT OUR COMMENTATOR

Roger G. Kennedy is Director Emeritus of the National Museum of American History, Smithsonian Institution. He is the former Director of the U.S. National Park Service, and during the 1970s served as Vice President of the Arts and of Finance for the Ford Foundation. In the 1950s, between three stints in the Eisenhower administration—as Special Assistant to the Secretary of Labor, to the Secretary of Health, Education and Welfare, and to the Attorney General—he was a White House correspondent for NBC. He later headed a commission for President Carter, served on another for President George H.W. Bush, and was appointed to the directorship of the National Park Service by President Clinton.

Like John Kennedy (who is no relation), Roger Kennedy served in the U.S. Navy in the Pacific theater. Although he played touch football with Senator Kennedy and his brothers in the 1950s—"on a patch of turf on P Street in Washington"—he gained a closer perspective of JFK in the 1970s, while serving under McGeorge Bundy, who was then president of the Ford Foundation. Bundy had been national security adviser to JFK.

During his fourteen-year tenure at the Smithsonian, Mr. Kennedy edited the twelve volumes of *The Smithsonian Guide to Historic America* and the reissue of *The WPA Guide to Washington, D.C.* He is also the author of books on Aaron Burr and Thomas Jefferson, three books on architectural history, and two, scheduled for publication in 2009, on the arts of the New Deal period.

ACKNOWLEDGMENTS

From Roger Kennedy go thanks to Berl Bernhard, David Ginsberg, James O. Horton, Lois Horton, Thomas Hughes, David Kennedy, Frances Kennedy, Nick Kotz, Harry McPherson, Paul Saffo, Hedrick Smith, James Symington, Harris Wofford, and John Zentay.

Levenger is indebted to the staff of the JFK Presidential Library for welcoming us into their archives. We would like to thank, in particular, Michael Desmond, Maryrose Grossman, and the ever-gracious Stephen Plotkin.

We also extend our thanks to Larry Ford and Wayne Welch for believing in this book from the beginning.

CONCORDANCE CLOUD

On the endpapers, you will find another way to depict JFK's Inaugural Address: a typographical concordance generated by viewing many of his key spoken words as data. The words in this concordance cloud are arranged sequentially, in order of utterance. The size of the word indicates the frequency with which JFK used it. You'll notice that the words *we* and *us* are the largest, hewing to JFK's desire to minimize the use of *I*.

Related words were categorized within their root words. *Freedom* is contained in *free, beginning* in *begin, renewal* in *renew, powers* and *powerful* in *power, revolutionary* in *revolution, rights* and *rightly* in *right, Americans* in *America, peaceful* in *peace, national* in *nation,* and *asking* in *ask.*

We welcome your comments on this concordance cloud, and on your experience of this multimedia book. Please visit this book's page on Levenger.com and click on the "Write a review" link.

CITIZENS WE FREE BEGIN RENEW

I GOD CENTURY WORLD POWER

REVOLUTION GLOBE RIGHT FRIEND FOE

GENERATION AMERICA WAR PEACE

NATION COMMITTED US PLEDGE LOYALTY

HELP ALLIANCE JOIN SCIENCE MANKIND

EXPLORE ENDEAVOR COUNTRY HISTORY ASK

UNCOMMON BOOKS
FOR SERIOUS READERS

CITIZENS WE

I GOD CENTURY W

REVOLUTION GLOBE

GENERATION AM

NATION COMMITTED U

HELP ALLIANCE

EXPLORE ENDEAVOR COU